Better Cocktails Through Chemistry:

A Guide to Sugar Free Drinks

Scott Reba

To Holly, for believing in me and always bringing out my better self.

CONTENTS

BETTER COCKTAILS THROUGH CHEMISTRY

ACKNOWLEDGMENTS

There are many people without whom this book would not exist, and I thank you for all your kind words and support throughout this process. Thank you to my father who's consultation on the chemical extraction process was key. I'd like to thank my wife, Holly, who I owe more to than words can ever describe. I'd also like to thank Jason Wisnieski, my lifelong friend, who gave me the initial idea and inspiration for this book, and supplied many spirits along the way. Thank you all for your taste-testing palettes, good times, and your friendship.

Special thanks to Jay Santini, who proofread this book and to Victoria Stanbridge of Victoria Stanbridge Photography for the awesome cover art and design.

Forward

For many years, I did not participate in certain aspects of social functions. There would be get-togethers, parties, and weddings, and people would do as people do and socialize over a cocktail. However, this was not an option for me. I have been a Type 1 diabetic (T1DM) since I was 13 years old. For over 25 years, I have learned to avoid sugar like the plague and, over time, have even limited food carbohydrates. This practice has allowed me to lower my HbA1c and virtually erase the peaks and valleys of my blood sugars. This better control has allowed me to live a healthier life free of complications from my disease.

This practice left me on the sidelines when it came to cocktails, though. Sure, I could sit and drink my rum and Diet Coke or sip my scotch, but I was missing out on mixed drinks. Much like a good meal, a good cocktail has flavor profiles, aromatics, and subtle complexities. The art of cocktail making is simply incredible. It also happened to be something closed off to me.

Saccharine in soda can be unpleasant, but is a necessary evil. Saccharine in a cocktail ruins the flavor and almost makes it unrecognizable compared to traditional recipe cocktails. It is also impossible to bake with. The world of sugar free cooking has changed dramatically over the years, but most recently with the introduction of Splenda, things changed for the better. Splenda, or sucralose, is an artificial sweetener that engages the same receptors on your tongue that indicate sweetness, yet has no calories or carbohydrates due to its molecular composition. It is not broken down, nor absorbed by the body. While this was useful for adding a little sweetness to my tea, it would be a while yet before it would mean something else to me.

A good friend of mine is a cocktail enthusiast and would always host a Repeal Day party every December to celebrate the repeal of prohibition of alcohol in the United States. I would, as mentioned above, not really participate in the tasting of various libations. One of those years, I had the inspiration to get up and try to do something about it and make actual sugar free, no carbohydrate versions of regular cocktails that tasted as close to the originals as possible. That being said, every good cocktail uses all natural ingredients. This presented various challenges, which over time and experimentation, were overcome to great success. My friend would give me a recipe, then we would test each drink side by side with regular cocktails versus sucralose sweetened cocktails and tweak recipes where necessary to make them as indistinguishable as possible. Eventually, we started running low on recipes since new recipes required sugar-infused spirits like cordials, vermouth, or liqueurs. This led me to research and invent ways to make my own homemade sugar free versions to open up those different families of cocktails. I started a website to document that journey and am now pleased to share all the various cocktails, liqueurs, and the processes that I invented to make this all possible in one convenient reference book.

Enjoy!

The following is a simple list of the different cocktails contained within this book that require a certain type of base components. Pure distilled spirits contain no sugar nor carbohydrates. The required liqueurs listed can all be made following the recipes in this book.

This list should make it easier to locate new cocktails that contain components that you've already made or obtained.

Not included in this list are bitters, ReaLemon, nor ReaLime. Almost every cocktail has a citrus component. Many require bitters. ReaLemon, ReaLime, and bitters are items that cocktail maker should always have in stock.

The most common bitters used are Angostura. They can be bought just about anywhere. Specialty bitters can be found online, or at your local liquor store for reasonably cheap, so plan ahead before making cocktails that require those.

Cocktails Sorted by Required Spirits

Absinthe
Deep Sea Cocktail
Royale with Ease
Sazerac
Gold Cup (Clio Version)

Allspice Dram
Royale with Ease
Lion's Tail
Nannie Dee

Pumpkin Spice Cocktail
Solstice
Woody Sour

Amaro
Alto Cucina
Apparent Sour
Good Night, Irene
Gruff and Rumble
Trans-Siberian Express

Apple Brandy (Applejack)
Carolina Julep
Gold Baron
Hawaiian Room
Pink Lady
Pioneer Spirit
Special Relationship

Brandy/Cognac
Charles Cocktail
Coquito
Curacao Punch
Gazette
Hot Toddy
Metropole
Mississippi Punch
Panama
Stinger

Crème de Cacao
Panama
Trans-Siberian Express
Grasshopper
Hershey Manhattan
Mulata Daisy

Crème de Menthe
Trans-Siberian Express
Grasshopper
Stinger

Crème de Violette
Aviation
Blue Moon

Fool Moon
Goodnight Gracie
Margarita Violette

Elderflower Cordial
Alto Cucina
Apparent Sour
Bohemian
Means of Preservation

Gin
Army & Navy
Aviation
Basil Gin Gimlet
Blue Moon
Deep Sea Cocktail
Fool Moon
Hong Kong Cocktail
Magnolia Blossom
Means of Preservation
Pink Lady
Ramos Gin Fizz
Tom Collins
Trans-Siberian Express

Grenadine
Angostura Fizz
Black Rose
Castle Habour Special
Chinese Cocktail
El Presidente
Gold Baron
Magnolia Blossom
Mexican Firing Squad
Opening Cocktail
Pink Lady

Grenadine (cont.)
Planters Punch
Scofflaw

Hibiscus Syrup
Royale with Ease
Wild Hibiscus Sour

Maraschino Liqueur
Aviation
Chinese Cocktail
Gold Cup (Clio Version)
Tango 'til They're Sore

Orgeat Syrup
Army & Navy
Gold Cup (Clio Version)
Pioneer Spirit
Trinidad Sour
Pineapple Vodka
Castle Habour Special
Panama
Saint Croix Rum Fix
Wild Hibiscus Sour

Rum (Spiced or Dark)
Castle Habour Special
Chinese Cocktail
Conquistador
El Presidente
Mississippi Punch
Saint Croix Rum Fix

Rum (White)
Castle Habour Special
Curacao Punch
Daiquiri
Gold Cup (Clio)
Goodnight Gracie
Gruff and Rumble
Hawaiian Room
Imperial Fizz
Mojito
Mulata Daisy
Panama
Planters Punch

Simple Syrup
Angostura Fizz
Buster Brown
Carolina Julep
Conquistador
Daiquiri
Fool Moon
Gold Cup (Clio Version)
Goodnight Gracie
Hong Kong Cocktail
Lion's Tail
Mark Twain Cocktail
Metropole
Planters Punch
Sazerac
Special Relationship
Tom Collins
Whiskey Sour
Woody Sour

Tequila
Conquistador
Margarita
Margarita Violette
Mexican Firing Squad
Paloma

Triple Sec
Chinese Cocktail
Curacao Punch
El Presidente
Gruff and Rumble
Hawaiian Room
Margarita
Margarita Violette
Solstice

Vermouth (Dry)
Alto Cucina
Deep Sea Cocktail
El Presidente
Hong Kong Cocktail
Means of Preservation
Metropole
Scofflaw
Smoky Grove

Vermouth (Sweet)
Charles
Gazette
Hershey Manhattan
Mulata Daisy
Opening Cocktail
Smoky Grove
Tango 'til They're Sore

Whiskey (Blended)
Imperial Fizz
Nannie Dee
Opening Cocktail
Pioneer Spirit

Whiskey (Bourbon)
Black Rose
Buster Brown
Coquito
Egg Nog
Gold Baron
Good Night, Irene
Hershey Manhattan
Lion's Tail
Mississippi Punch
Old Fashioned
Pumpkin Spice Cocktail
Special Relationship
Whiskey Sour
Wild Hibiscus Sour
Woody Sour

Whiskey (Rye)
Carolina Julep
Old Fashioned
Sazerac
Scofflaw
Solstice
Special Relationship
Tango 'til They're Sore
Trinidad Sour
Woody Sour

Whiskey (Scotch)

Alto Cucina
Mark Twain Cocktail
Smoky Grove
Special Relationship

Sugar Free Base Spirit and Liqueur Recipes

Allspice Dram (Pimento Dram)

Source: Seriouseats.com for providing the original inspiration.

This is an older liqueur that in classic cocktails is also referred to as a Pimento Dram. The Allspice Dram is a complex, yet spicy, addition to many drinks. There are very few commercially available brands. There is the St. Elizabeth Allspice Dram or the Bitter Truth Pimento Dram. There was a time when it was totally unavailable in the United States and was strictly a product of the Caribbean. With the resurgence of tiki drinks, the Allspice Dram has become more accessible. The Sugar Free Allspice Dram can also be easily made at home. However, Splenda Brown Sugar does contain trace amounts of carbohydrates (about 2 grams per serving). Since most cocktails that utilize the Allspice Dram call for an average of 0.5 ounces of dram, it is so negligible in carb content that it may as well be zero. If this is unacceptable and you want absolutely zero carbs/sugars, regular Splenda can be used but will require 2/3 of a cup instead of the half cup of the brown sugar blend. Keep in mind that this will also slightly change the flavor profile of the dram once it is finished and will lack the caramelized sugar flavor.

continued

Ingredients:
- 1 cup Light Rum
- 1/4 cup Whole Allspice Berries
- 1 Cinnamon Stick
- 1 1/2 cups Water
- 1/2 cup Splenda Brown Sugar Blend

Optional Step: It is highly recommended that you toast the allspice berries prior to starting out, though this is not essential. It will bring out richer flavors by toasting them beforehand. Skip the baking step below if you wish to omit this step (again, not recommended).

Preheat your oven to 350.° When up to temperature, put the allspice berries in a baking-safe bowl and place in the oven for 10 minutes. Then, crush the allspice berries with a mortar and pestle. It should be a rough grind, with just enough crushing to break up the dried berries but not completely pulverize them into powder. You want to see broken bits of berries. Next, find a glass container that can be sealed. Place the crushed allspice berries inside and add the rum. Seal the lid, give it a swirl, then put it in a cool, dark place and walk away. Record the date and time for reference.

Agitate once a day for 5 days. On day 5, open the container and crack one stick of cinnamon over the allspice/rum mixture and drop all pieces into the mix. Reseal the container, agitate, and then put it back in its cool, dark place. Agitate daily for an additional 7 days (12 days of total steep time). After the steeping is over, multiple filtration steps will be required to remove the bits and pieces of allspice berries and cinnamon.

Use a simple wire strainer to remove the larger chunks, and then strain again once the original strainer is cleaned out. Then strain a third time with a coffee filter. If you have a food grade funnel, use it to hold the coffee filter, as it creates less mess and less loss of dram.

Once filtered, gently heat the 1.5 cups of water, but do not let it boil. Then add the Splenda of choice. Gently mix until the powder is completely dissolved, then remove from the heat. Allow to cool for a bit, as you don't want to add the alcohol to a hot liquid. Once cool, mix the alcohol with the syrup, pour into a bottle (I recommend a dark bottle to reduce light infiltration), and label with the date.

Amaro

Source: Adapted from Seriouseats.com, who published their DIY version.

Amaro is an herbal liqueur that is commonly imbibed as an after-dinner digestif. Early on, digestifs were theorized to aid in the digestive process. There are several other digestifs other than Amaro, like brandy/cognac, or fortified wines like sherry and port.

Amaro contains many different herbs and can be quite bitter. It is also important to stress that Amaro is a category of liqueur, and many different brands have many different flavor profiles, so when making a cocktail with it, it is important to match the Amaro spirit specified to best mimic the drink. After some tasting comparisons with commercial brands, this sugar free version of Amaro most closely resembles Cynar in its flavor profile.

Note: Amaro will take around a month to bring to completion. Also, the recipe below can easily be halved. If you are curious, you may dip a spoon in once a week or so to taste the Sugar Free Amaro as the different flavor profiles emerge. It is amazing how it changes over time. Be warned, it will be bitter and strong! This is normal, and you should not be worried!

(continued)

Ingredients:
- 1 tspn Anise Seed
- 6 fresh Sage Leaves
- 6 fresh Mint Leaves
- 1 tspn Fresh Rosemary Leaves
  (about 1 sprig's worth)
- Allspice Berry
- 1/2 tspn Whole Cloves
- 1/2 tspn Gentian Root
- 3 cups Everclear 151 (75% Ethanol)*
- 1 1/4 cups Splenda
- 1 1/4 Water

Lightly grind all the herbs and spices with a mortar and pestle in order to express the oils within. Transfer all the crushed herbs to a sealable glass container and pour the alcohol in, which should cover all the ground ingredients. Now store in a cool, dark place for 3 weeks, agitating once a day.

Once the mixture has steeped for 3 weeks, make a sugar free simple syrup by taking the Splenda and dissolving it in the water. Heating is unnecessary in this step, as Splenda dissolves easily in water.

Now add the sugar free simple syrup to the herb/alcohol mix. Reseal the container and place back into a cool and dark location and allow to steep for an additional 7 days, agitating daily (Optional: If a stronger flavor is desired, steep for up to two more weeks.)

Now strain the mixture through some cheesecloth, and then filter again through some fresh cheesecloth for a second straining, or use a coffee filter. Pour slowly, as clogs can happen and more than one filter may be required.

Store at room temperature for up to six months (possibly longer in the fridge).

*Warning: Using high proof food-grade grain alcohol (Everclear) can be dangerous. It is highly flammable and should never be imbibed by itself as inebriation can happen very quickly and much faster than one would expect. Everclear is odorless and tasteless, which makes it ideal for our purposes, but makes it dangerous to leave unattended around animals or minors. Never use laboratory grade alcohol as a substitute. It can contain methanol that is highly toxic and potentially fatal. If you only have access to the higher proof 191, just substitute 3/4 cup of 191-Everclear plus 1/4 cup water for every cup of 151-proof required.

Creme de Cacao

It was first mentioned in a French cookbook in the 1600s and more reliably published in the 1800s. It should also be noted that when Creme is referenced, it does not mean a dairy cream, but refers to the texture of the liqueur. Some other examples are Creme de Violette or Creme de Menthe. Another note is that this preparation is not 100% no carb, though the carb content is still negligible. The cocoa used contains 3 grams of carbohydrates per tablespoon. This recipe calls for 1/4 cup of cocoa, which equals 12 grams of total carbohydrates in this preparation. However, since much of this cocoa is eventually strained out after flavor extraction, and it is then further diluted into almost 4 cups of liquid, even if it were to retain all of its carbs, it would work out to 0.375 grams of carbs per ounce. After all the filtration steps, we estimate the carbohydrate amount is so minute as to call it sugar free, but we can't rule out some carbohydrate contamination.

Ingredients:
- 1.5 cups Everclear 151 (75% Ethanol)*
- 1/2 tspn Vanilla Extract
- 1/4 cup Cocoa
- 2 cups Splenda
- 2 cups (total) Water

Measure out the cocoa and place it in a sealable glass dish. Now, take the Everclear-151 and slowly pour it over the powdered cocoa. Add the Vanilla Extract. Then seal up the bowl and agitate carefully. Set it aside for 24 hours in a dark location. Once the day has elapsed, make a simple 2:1 syrup by taking 2 cups of Splenda and adding it to 1+1/3 cups of water. This should go into solution rather easily, but if it does not, gently heat it until it dissolves entirely, making sure to remove it from the heat and allow to cool before the next step. Slowly filter the cocoa infused alcohol through a coffee filter. It is advised to place the filter in a funnel and collect what comes through into a cup/bottle. There is a likelihood that the first filter may clog, which is why slowly pouring is important. If that happens, carefully remove the old filter and put a new one in and repeat until all the liquid is through. Carefully squeeze the filter to try and get every drop of flavor out. Measure the volume of the resulting filtered cocoa-infused alcohol. If it is less than 1.5 cups, add back enough Everclear-151 to bring it back up to the original volume. Now add 1/2 cup of water plus 2 cups of the previously made Splenda 2:1 syrup.

You can drink this right away, but it is advisable to let it rest for up to a week beforehand to let the flavors meld. The final proof of the Sugar Free Creme de Cacao is 50.

*Warning: Using high proof food-grade grain alcohol (Everclear) can be dangerous. It is highly flammable and should never be imbibed by itself as inebriation can happen very quickly and much faster than one would expect. Everclear is odorless and tasteless, which makes it ideal for our purposes, but makes it dangerous to leave unattended around animals or minors. Never use laboratory grade alcohol as a substitute. It can contain methanol that is highly toxic and potentially fatal. If you only have access to the higher proof 191, just substitute 3/4 cup of 191-Everclear plus 1/4 cup water for every cup of 151-proof required.

Creme de Menthe

Source: Serious Eats

Creme de Menthe is an ingredient that is used in many older cocktails. Several versions of it exist, including white and green creme de menthe, but they are really just the same thing with different coloring. That being said, many creme de menthes are made using extracts or by adding green food coloring. We directly compared this sugar free version to two commercial versions, one from DeKuyper and the other from Tempus Fugit. The Tempus Fugit (which was distilled and colorless) was a much more balanced liqueur and tasted the most like our product.

Ingredients:
- 1.5 cups Fresh Mint Leaves
- 1.5 cups Splenda
- 2 cups Water
- 1 cup Everclear 151 (75% Ethanol)*
- Green Food Coloring**

First, separate the mint leaves from the stems until you have a full cup of leaves only. Then tear up those leaves into quarters and place them in a sealable glass bowl, preferably a shallow one. Then add the Everclear and seal the top. Gently swirl the mint in the alcohol, and then place in a dark, cool place for 12 hours.

After the 12-hour steep, strain out the mint leaves with a strainer, making sure to keep all the alcohol. Discard those mint leaves and return the mint-infused alcohol back to the original bowl. Separate a 1/2-cup of mint leaves from the stems and again tear into quarters and place them into the mint-infused alcohol.

Gently mix and allow to steep in a dark, cool place for 10 to 12 hours.

After the second steep, strain out the mint leaves with the same strainer, then strain the alcohol a second time through either cheesecloth or a coffee filter. Once filtered, add the water and the Splenda. Gently mix until the Splenda dissolves. This process should not require heat since Splenda is very water soluble. Please keep out of direct light to reduce the browning of the mixture due to the chlorophyll from the mint.

*Warning: Using high proof food-grade grain alcohol (Everclear) can be dangerous. It is highly flammable and should never be imbibed by itself as inebriation can happen very quickly and much faster than one would expect. Everclear is odorless and tasteless, which makes it ideal for our purposes, but makes it dangerous to leave unattended around animals or minors. Never use laboratory grade alcohol as a substitute. It can contain methanol that is highly toxic and potentially fatal. If you only have access to the higher proof 191, just substitute 3/4 cup of 191-Everclear plus 1/4 cup water for every cup of 151-proof required.

**If you want the ultra bright green color to last, keep it in the dark, but it will eventually turn brownish no matter how the liqueur is stored. The chlorophyll that comes from the mint leaves will quickly break down when exposed to light. If desired, adding some green food coloring will help bring the original bright green color back. If you want to go this route, slowly add drops of green food coloring until the desired color is reached, but be extra careful not to spill!

Creme de Violette
(aka Creme Yvette in older recipes)

The Sugar Free Creme de Violette is another unique innovation! Liqueurs and cordials are largely undiscovered territories for sugar free and no carb cocktails due to the sugar gradient extraction processes and addition of sugar afterwards that exists in commercial brands. To further complicate things for the Sugar Free Creme de Violette and all the older recipes, the regular sugary version was simply unavailable in the United States for decades. However, in 2007, an Austrian company named Rothman and Winter started producing and exporting Creme de Violette. We did a side-by-side taste test comparison and, while the Sugar Free version had a slightly different texture, its color and flavor are very similar. A brief word of warning though, in order to achieve the same colors, we had to use food coloring. Please be careful of spillage when drinking any of the Sugar Free Creme de Violette, lest some staining occur!

Ingredients:
- 25 grams Blue Violet Leaf (*Viola odorata)*
- 1.5 cups Everclear 151 (75% Ethanol)*
- 0.5 cup Splenda
- 1.25 cups Water
- 30 drops Blue Food Coloring
- 20 drops Red Food Coloring

Simply measure out your Blue Violet Leaf (yes, that was grams above, so switch your kitchen scale over to metric for this) and place it in a sealable glass bowl. Add the Everclear and make sure that the Blue Violet Leaf is completely submerged. Seal the lid and place in a darkened area at room temperature for 48 hours. Make sure to give it a swirl a couple times a day.

After the solution is done steeping, note the color. It's green! This is normal, and you should not be worried. Take your blue violet infused alcohol and strain out as much of the particulate as possible by squeezing it through some cheese cloth. Now filter it a second time through a standard coffee filter. It is recommended to place a funnel into the final collecting bottle and strain the infused alcohol right in. Less transfer equals less waste. Once the infused alcohol is done filtering, remove the coffee filter and add the Splenda, water, and food coloring.

*Warning: Using high proof food-grade grain alcohol (Everclear) can be dangerous. It is highly flammable and should never be imbibed by itself as inebriation can happen very quickly and much faster than one would expect. Everclear is odorless and tasteless, which makes it ideal for our purposes, but makes it dangerous to leave unattended around animals or minors. Never use laboratory grade alcohol as a substitute. It can contain methanol that is highly toxic and potentially fatal. If you only have access to the higher proof 191, just substitute 3/4 cup of 191-Everclear plus 1/4 cup water for every cup of 151-proof required.

Elderflower Cordial

Source: SeriousEats.com.

Elderflower cordials have a long history, and while elderberries do come from the same plant, please do not mistake this for an elderberry cordial! The Sugar Free Elderflower Cordial is surprisingly easy to make and relatively inexpensive as well. We did our very best to replicate the sweetness and coloring of the famous St. Germain, including the sweetness to volume, color, as well as the alcohol content (40 proof). However, due to the presence of Splenda, like all Splenda sweetened liqueurs and cordials, it is slightly cloudy. Our Sugar Free Elderflower Cordial tasted very close to the St. Germain. It did lack a little of the mouth-feel of St. Germain, but that is also a limitation of the Splenda system as well.

Ingredients:
- 1/2 Orange Rind*
- 1/3 Lemon Rind*
- 2+1/3 cups Water
- 2 cups Splenda
- 2/3 cup Everclear 151 (75% Ethanol)**
- 1/4 cup Dried Elderflowers
- 1.5 tspn Citric Acid Powder

Take the lemon and orange peels, the dried elderflowers, and the Everclear and place in a sealable glass dish. Make sure that all the dry ingredients are covered/saturated with the alcohol, then seal and place in a cool, dark place.

Allow steeping for 24 hours, then open up the container and remove the lemon and orange peels and discard. If possible, place in some cheesecloth and wring out any alcohol that was absorbed into the peels. Reseal, then agitate the remains and return to that cool dark place.

Steep for 48 more hours (Day 3); add the citric acid, making sure to stir the solution until the citric acid is completely dissolved. Reseal the bowl and place back in your favorite cool and dark place.

Steep for 24 more hours (Day 4), get a bowl and a strainer, preferably one that sits easily within the bowl, and line it with cheesecloth. Carefully pour the alcohol and elderflower into the cheesecloth. Now wrap up the remaining elderflower caught in the cheesecloth and wring it out in order to remove as much of the infused alcohol from the elderflower as possible. In a separate bowl, mix the water and the Splenda.^ Once the Splenda is completely dissolved, measure out 1/2 cup of the elderflower infused alcohol and add them together.

You may want to run the solution through a coffee filter to further strain out any potential particulates, but this is not required. Store in the refrigerator.

*We used a swivel peeler to remove only the top layer of the rind. Try, at all costs, not to go down too deep, as the flesh under the rind is rather bitter.

**Warning: Using high proof food-grade grain alcohol (Everclear) can be dangerous. It is highly flammable and should never be imbibed by itself as inebriation can happen very quickly and much faster than one would expect. Everclear is odorless and tasteless, which makes it ideal for our purposes, but makes it dangerous to leave unattended around animals or minors. Never use laboratory grade alcohol as a substitute. It can contain methanol that is highly toxic and potentially fatal. If you only have access to the higher proof 191, just substitute 3/4 cup of 191-Everclear plus 1/4 cup water for every cup of 151-proof required.

^You may want to pre-warm the water in the microwave for up to a minute. You do not want the water hot, but warming it up a little will help the Splenda dissolve a little easier. It may not be necessary, however, depending on the original temperature of the water.

Grenadine

Grenadine is a pretty common ingredient in classic cocktails. Grenadine is used in many Shirley Temple cocktails, as well as a tasty add-on to many regular cocktails that add a sweet and refreshing flavor. Grenadine is basically just syrup of pomegranate juice and sugar, so making it at home is cheap and easy. However, since juices contain carbohydrates and sugars, one can never be completely no carb/no sugar, but modern science has helped. At your local grocer, pick up some Diet Oceanspray blueberry/pomegranate juice for this recipe. It has only 2 grams of carbohydrates per 8 fluid ounces, and as the recipe calls for a quart, which is 4 cups, and one cup weighs 8 ounces, then there are only 8 grams of carbs in the whole recipe! As cocktails that call for Grenadine usually only require an ounce at a time, that's really only 0.25 grams of carbohydrates per serving. That is low enough to pass our standards. The blueberry add-on doesn't overtly change the flavor or the coloring either. Unless you were told, you'd probably never know there was blueberry lurking in this sugar free grenadine recipe!

Ingredients:
- 1 Quart Diet OceanSpray Blueberry/Pomegranate Juice
- 2 cups Splenda
- 2 dashes Orange Flower Water
- 1 oz Vodka (Optional)

Warm up the juice on the stove, but stop heating

(continued)

23

before it boils. Add the Splenda and allow it to dissolve. Take off the heat and allow the syrup to cool. Add the Orange Flower Water and store either at room temperature or refrigerate.

Optional: Adding the vodka does not change the flavor, but provides a little bit of anti-bacterial protection.

Hibiscus Simple Syrup

The Sugar Free Hibiscus Simple Syrup is an uncommon specialty syrup. Making this can be difficult, as getting the hibiscus can be challenging. Not all variations of the hibiscus flower are edible, and most of the wild/garden varieties are inedible. Some stores stock fresh edible hibiscus flowers, but not really in my part of the US. When I made mine, I found dried hibiscus flowers at my local organic grocery store. It's also a good bet that there are other tea shops or organic food stores that sell the dried version, but be warned that it should be pure hibiscus and not mixed with anything else at all. I used the same weight of dried hibiscus as fresh, which may have altered the flavor a little, but the flavor is subtle either way and, like grenadine, it is used just as much for coloring as for flavoring.

Ingredients:
- 2.75 cups Water^
- 2 cups Splenda
- 0.5 oz (by weight) Dried Hibiscus Flowers
- Reusable Tea Bag
- 1 oz Vodka (optional)

Boil the water and add the Splenda until it dissolves. While making the syrup, add the pre-weighed hibiscus to the bag, cinch it closed, and then add the bag to the lightly boiling syrup. Stir occasionally for a total steep time of 10 minutes. Remove the bag, allow to cool, and then pour into a bottle and store.

(continued)

The result should be a syrup with a beautiful blood-red coloring.

Optional: Add 1 oz of vodka to the finished product to act as an anti-bacterial agent.

^As a side-note, remember that the water displacement of Splenda is different than sugar, which is why there appears to be more water than should be necessary for a simple 1:1 syrup.

Maraschino Liqueur

After a fair bit of research on Maraschino Liqueur, we found that it requires marasca cherry pits, which are bitter, as opposed to the standard grocery store cherries and are used during the distillation phase in order to extract some of those flavors. Finding dried marasca cherry pits is quite an ordeal and honestly, not one that I was able to successfully complete. However, I did eventually find a website that sold regular dried cherry pits called The Cherry Pit Store. This Sugar Free Maraschino Liqueur packs a little bit more cherry flavor than that of its cousin, Luxardo. This is mostly due to the fact that our process does not distill our extract; so many of the aromatics that may be removed during the distillation process have not been used. That being said, if a recipe calls for Luxardo or Maraschino Liqueur, you may want to halve what is called for and do a simple taste test before proceeding.

Ingredients:
- 2 cups Dried Cherry Pits
- 2+ cups Everclear 151 (75% Ethanol)*
- Water (as needed to dilute 1:2)
- Splenda (.322 tablespoons per final volume)
- Digital Balance

First, measure out the two cups of dried cherry pits and put in a sealable glass container. Then pour the Everclear over the dried cherry pits until they are barely covered. Depending on the size of your container, this may vary. Note, using too much Everclear will just cause the cherry pits to float. You want as much surface contact between the ethanol and the cherry pits as possible, so use as little as you can, as long as everything is covered. I used a bowl that nested into my bigger bowl to submerge the pits. *Then seal the container and store in a dark cupboard.*

Pull it out once a day and stir the cherry pits, resealing and placing back in the cupboard, for 7 days total.

On the 7th day, pour out the cherry pit-infused alcohol through a mesh strainer. We recommend one with a handle that can hang over a collection bowl for ease. Pro Tip: Pre-weigh or tare your collection device. You'll notice that the amount of volume of cherry pit-infused alcohol is much less than when you started, as the cherry pits will absorb some of the alcohol. Weigh the liquid you collected in ounces. Whatever weight you have collected, double it with water. (For example, if you collect 6.3 ounces of alcohol, add back 6.3 ounces of water for a final weight of 12.6 ounces of fluid.) This reduces the alcohol content down to ~32% (64 proof). Now strain through a coffee filter and a funnel, or pour through cheesecloth to remove any particulate. Re-weigh the contents and add 0.322 tablespoons of Splenda per ounce of fluid. (For example, 12.6 fluid ounces x 0.322 = just a hair over 4 tablespoons.) You'll want to be fairly close, only to keep the sweetness profile similar between a regular name brand Maraschino Liqueur. Refrigerate.

*Warning: Using high proof food-grade grain alcohol (Everclear) can be dangerous. It is highly flammable and should never be imbibed by itself as inebriation can happen very quickly and much faster than one would expect. Everclear is odorless and tasteless, which makes it ideal for our purposes, but makes it dangerous to leave unattended around animals or minors. Never use laboratory grade alcohol as a substitute. It can contain methanol that is highly toxic and potentially fatal. If you only have access to the higher proof 191, just substitute 3/4 cup of 191-Everclear plus 1/4 cup water for every cup of 151-proof required.

Milk Substitutes

Since the goal is to be no (or as low) carb as possible, using milk in a cocktail can be problematic. Heavy whipping cream can be substituted. Other good options are unsweetened coconut milk or unsweetened almond milk. Dissolve 1 teaspoon of Splenda into 4 ounces (1 cup) to any of them to bring them back to the equivalent sweetness of milk.

Orgeat Syrup

Unless you fortify this with Splenda and a couple ounces of vodka, it won't last more than a week. Even fortified, it is a good idea to shake the syrup vigorously at least every couple days, otherwise it will separate. The shelf life for Orgeat Syrup is about a month at the longest, even refrigerated. This, unfortunately, is normal for the regular sugary version as well.

Ingredients:
- Water
- 1 cup Almonds (can be scaled for how much you want to make)
- Splenda
- Vodka
- Cheesecloth
- Rose Water
- Orange Flower Water
- Bitter Almond Extract (optional)

*First, blanch the almonds to remove their skin, or buy blanched almonds (alternately, leave the skin on; this changes the color/flavor a bit, and some people prefer that). Coarsely chop one cup of almonds. Put the almonds in a bowl and fill with enough water to cover. Let sit 1/2 hour at room temperature, and then **discard the water**.*

*Return almonds to a bowl and cover with one cup of water. Let it sit for one hour. Place some coarse cheesecloth in a strainer, and squeeze out the water, **saving** the liquid this time. Squeeze as much water as you can out of the almonds, again, reserving the liquid. When done, return the almonds to the liquid, and let sit for another hour. Repeat the* *straining, squeezing, and reserving. Optionally, return the almonds to the liquid for a third hour and repeat the straining one last time.*

The result is almond milk. To make the Orgeat syrup, measure the volume of almond milk, then use this as the base for a 1:1 syrup with one cup of Splenda over light heat per cup of almond milk, stirring constantly until the sugar is dissolved. Do not let simmer!

When cool, add a few drops of rose water, orange flower water, and, if desired, a drop of bitter almond extract (all to taste). We recommend doing this when cool to make sure the aromatics don't immediately evaporate.

This makes about 1.5 cups of syrup. Remember, Orgeat separates as the solids and fats come out of suspension with the water and other liquids. This is normal—shake every day or two to get the most out of your syrup.

ReaLemon and ReaLime: A Comparison to Actual Juice

In our early research, we taste tested a simple sugar into water versus Splenda into ReaLemon for tartness versus sweetness. Once we determined that optimal ratio, we assumed that ReaLime would require the same ratio, but this was not the case. ReaLime is a little more limey than a normal fresh lime. Drinks are always to taste, and we encourage you to try mixing the drinks with slightly different proportions if what you try isn't quite to your liking. In the case of the ReaLime, it seems that, per serving, it is almost twice as much lime flavor per volume. So we've started using a half ReaLime, half water version when a recipe calls for lime juice. All posted recipes use our ReaLime 50:50 mix. However, if you like lime, feel free to go all out, but use caution. It doesn't take much to throw the balance of a drink off, and it's much easier to add more of something than to remove it.

Simple Syrup

Generally, whenever an old recipe calls for powdered sugar, what they mean in modern standards is traditional granulated sugar. Refined sugar was much harder to get in the old days and often required clarifying, which it no longer does. Please keep that in mind if you try to compare the following recipe with an older version that you might find elsewhere. You can also scale up this recipe to make larger volumes.

Since this sugar free version does not actually contain sugar, it is more susceptible to bacterial/fungal contamination, so smaller batches won't be wasted as much if they do get contaminated. I like to add a shot of vodka to my syrup to help it keep longer without altering the flavor/sweetness too much.

Ingredients:
Gum Arabic Half:
- 1/4 cup Water
- 1/4 cup Gum Arabic (Acacia Powder)

Splenda Half:
- 1 cup Splenda
- 3/4 cup Water^

Heat the 1/4-cup water to the point where it's just starting to boil, and slowly, while stirring constantly, add the gum arabic. This will make a sticky mess, and you'll wonder what you just got yourself into. You may want to raise and lower the pot above the heat in order to more easily maintain a light boil. It's very easy to get to the full boil, and that's where the bubbly mess starts. No matter what you do, you'll probably end up with lumps. Take a spoon (metal—you may never get a wooden spoon clean), and keep stirring, and stirring. When you find lumps, break them up with the spoon. Here, you can trade time for effort. It's been my experience that you can be vigilant and smash all the lumps, and take about 15 minutes doing it. Or, you can take care of the worst offenders and get the mixture reasonably smooth, then just let it sit for a couple hours and let the water slowly work its way into the lumps (checking and breaking up the worst offenders as you go). The gum is done when it's no longer a gluey mass but a thick kind of molasses consistency.

Now make a simple 2:1 syrup: Put the 3/4-cup of water in a small pot. Set the heat on medium, and then add the Splenda. Stir constantly until everything dissolves, but make sure the total time on the heat is about 10 minutes. The mixture should never simmer, though it'll probably come close. You'll know when it is done when the surface gets a little bit of shimmer, but not a whole lot. It should be noted that it does not take very much heat to dissolve the Splenda, so keeping the solution on the heat for the full 10 minutes is important.^ Now pour in your gum mixture. Adding the now cool gum will take the temperature back down while you stir it in to dissolve. This time, the mixtures should go together much more easily than when the gum was a solid. It'll foam a bit though, especially as the mixture starts to simmer. You can utilize the floating pan trick mentioned above to lessen the foaming. Remove from heat and, using your metal spoon again, collect and discard as much of the foam as you can. It's sticky, like marshmallow foam, so the task isn't hard. Washing the spoon is easy with lots of hot water, or just soak it in slightly soapy water overnight before washing. Once everything is mixed, let cool, and bottle.

^While Splenda is volume-to-volume as sweet as sugar, its density and weight are much lower than sugar, which means that the water displacement is less when you solubilize it. I determined that the volume displacement difference was 0.4 cups for one cup in a 1:1 syrup. This means that after heating the water/Splenda mix until it is totally dissolved, you must add 0.4 cups of water afterwards to maintain the correct sweetness-to-volume ratio. Since we are making a 2:1 syrup, the correction volume is halved. One-quarter cup is close enough to 0.2 cups that it won't make much difference, but be careful how much rounding you do if you scale up the recipe. The reason this is added at the end, rather than during the heating process, is because the volume change correction takes into account the evaporation loss during the 10 minutes of heating.

Triple Sec

Loosely based on the general Thomas recipe.

Triple Sec, Cointreau, and Grand Marnier are all forms of orange liqueurs that were originally known as Curaçao. Curaçao Triple Sec was the original brand name of Curaçao, but somewhere along the way the Curaçao got dropped, and Triple Sec became the common nomenclature. The Cointreau and Grand Marnier versions are just name-brand versions of the same thing. Therefore, when coming across older recipes calling for an orange liqueur, it may state Curaçao, Triple Sec, Orange Liqueur, Cointreau, or Grand Marnier, but all of them can be used fairly interchangeably.

There are many recipes on the Internet on how to make homemade Triple Sec, but all of them use sugar gradients in order to extract the flavors from the orange. Our main goal is to make no carb, no sugar versions of drinks, so we used an alcohol gradient instead.

Orange rind, in and of itself, only contains 1 gram of carbohydrates per 6 grams of peel, so any sugar-soluble molecules will want to leave the peel and go into the solution. This process can be quickened by the application of heat. There are also other molecules that are only alcohol soluble. Most recipes you'll find online for making Triple Sec utilize these gradients to extract the oils and flavors from the peel. Then they'll supplement with juice for extra orangey flavor. This method ensures that all/most of the internal oils are extracted into the sugar solution. Fortunately, modern chemistry has something that our friends from the 1800s did not, namely, highly concentrated alcohol

that is biologically safe to imbibe, i.e., Everclear.*
High alcohol content gradients work just like a sugar gradient. This means that the oils and flavors stay in the peel until there is more liquid that they are soluble in outside of the peel. It effectively pulls them out like a magnet pulling metal filings out of a basket.

Upon taste testing our product against name brand versions, our Sugar Free Triple Sec is very similar to Cointreau and is very delicious. Please follow all safety guidelines mentioned below to prevent accidents. I also did extensive testing to ascertain how many carbohydrates came along for the ride during the extraction process. Ingesting one ounce on three separate occasions, I noticed no discernible changes in my blood sugar, so I'm willing to claim that the oranges retained most, if not all, of their original sugars.

Ingredients:
- 240 grams Orange Peel (about 6 #4014 Valencia oranges)
- ~3 cups of Everclear 151 (75% Ethanol)*
- ~3 cups 2:1 Splenda Syrup**
- Water

First, peel the oranges. When peeling your oranges, remove as much of the flesh under the rind as possible. Rinse the peels under running water to remove potential juice, and then blot dry. The flesh can carry bitter flavors, so get as much of the flesh off as you can. Once you have all the peels, cut them into narrow strips to increase surface area. Find a pot, with a matching lid, that is big enough to hold all the peels but narrow enough to completely cover the peels with 2.5 cups of 75% Everclear (you can easily test this by trying it with water first during the rinsing step). Add the Everclear to the pot, and then turn on the heat slowly. Only use an electric cooktop indoors and anything using flames outside! With an electric, we dialed it up to 8 until it just started bubbling, then down to 2–3 for 20 minutes, keeping it at a very low boil (75% ethanol boils at about 180° F.).

Make sure proper ventilation is used here. Breathing alcohol vapors can intoxicate you quickly. Please take proper safety measures, and do not use open flames anywhere during these steps, unless outside and with proper safety gear and fire extinguishers present. Steaming concentrated alcohol catches fire very easily.

Remove from heat and allow to cool with the lid on (prevents further evaporation). Now remove peels (saving them for later) and measure remaining volume of extract. We had 2 cups remaining of our starting 2.5 cups due to evaporation during the heating phase. Add appropriate volumes of 75% Everclear (in our case 1/2 cup) to bring the volume back up to the starting volume of 2.5 cups. Now place the liquid and the rinds in a glass, sealable container. We used a sealable glass bowl and placed a smaller glass bowl inside in order to make sure all peels were still submerged in the alcohol, as they tend to float. Seal the container and place in a dark area.

Agitate occasionally and incubate for a total of 24 hours at room temperature. After the steeping period, pour the orange-infused alcohol into a separate container and discard the peel. It is recommended, though not necessary, to now strain the liquid to remove any debris. However, not all debris will be removed, so some settling may occur in your end product. This is okay and normal. Swirl your bottle around prior to using in order to gently mix in order to redistribute the sediment.

Now measure the volume of alcohol. And here is where things get tricky and potentially dangerous, so take all precautions stated above. You'll want to reduce down your volume of alcohol by 34%. The goal here is to concentrate the orange flavors and to reduce the alcohol content of the final product, via evaporation, without overly diluting the flavors that were extracted. To reduce the volume of 2.5 cups by 34%, measure the volume, then place the alcohol on a heat source and bring up the temperature slowly. Measure often by pouring back and forth into a glass measuring cup. This liquid will be warm, so wear appropriate hand and body protection.

Follow all previous safety guidelines regarding heating alcohol! Your safety is at risk.

Once the volume is reduced by 34%, in our case, down to 1 and 2/3 cups, add back 5/6ths of a cup (1/2 cup + 1/3 cup) of water. If you accidentally over-evaporate, just add back the necessary amount of 75% Everclear to get the volume back to 1 and 2/3rd cups. Once the water is added, the final volume should be back to 2.5 cups, the original orange flavor retained, but now the final alcohol content of the solution should be 50%. This is, of course, too much (our target is 50 proof), so now add 2.5 cups of the 2:1 syrup,** which sweetens the final product and further reduces the alcohol content to 25%, or 50 proof. Now bottle and allow to rest for 24 hours. Store in a cool, dark place to retain color. You can sample a bit if you want, but the flavor does mature a little bit over time.

After resting, pour into a glass storage bottle and store in the refrigerator.

*Warning: Using high proof food-grade grain alcohol (Everclear) can be dangerous. It is highly flammable and should never be imbibed by itself as inebriation can happen very quickly and much faster than one would expect. Everclear is odorless and tasteless, which makes it ideal for our purposes, but makes it dangerous to leave unattended around animals or minors. Never use laboratory grade alcohol as a substitute. It can contain methanol that is highly toxic and potentially fatal. If you only have access to the higher proof 191, just substitute 3/4 cup of 191-Everclear plus 1/4 cup water for every cup of 151-proof required.

**2:1 Splenda syrup is different from the previously mentioned Sugar Free Simple Syrup. It is just a Splenda/water mixture. Take 4 cups of Splenda and dissolve into 3 cups water (this corrects for the volume displacement). It may take longer if using cold water to dissolve.

Vermouth (Dry)

Vermouth is technically in the class of being a fortified wine. Wine naturally contains sugars, which is a problem, and the procedure of fortifying wine adds even more. The first attempt at making our own sugar free vermouth was the Sweet Vermouth, so please refer to that recipe or visit mixdrinkrepeat.com for the backstory behind that recipe. Dry Vermouth is made using the same basic method, but with slightly different ingredients and a different amount of sweetness. Please keep in mind that many of the ingredients are measured in grams.

Ingredients:
- 2 grams Wormwood
- 2 grams Fresh Oregano
- 1/4 tspn dried Chamomile Flowers
- 1 Vanilla Bean, sliced down the center and opened up
- 1 gram Dried Orange Peel
- 1 sprig Fresh Sage
- 1 sprig Fresh Basil
- 1 sprig Fresh Thyme
- 1 tspn Cardamom Pods (crushed)
- 1/2 cup Everclear 151 (75% Ethanol) (plus a little extra for later)
- 1 cup E&J Brandy (recommended for end product flavor)
- 3.5 cups Water
- 1/4 cup Splenda
- 4.5 tspn Red Wine Vinegar (make sure to look at the label and verify that it's unsweetened)

First, crush the cardamom with a mortar and pestle. Then, place all the herbs, the crushed cardamom, and (continued) the orange peel in a glass bowl with a sealable top. Pour on the Everclear and gently macerate everything in the alcohol with a wooden spoon. Place the lid on the container and store in a dark location for 24 hours, shaking every few hours.

*Once the herbs are done steeping, pour everything into a cheesecloth-lined glass container and squeeze out all the liquid into a bowl. Measure the volume of the herb-infused alcohol. If it is less than the prerequisite 1/2 cup (*which it should be by a little)*, bring the volume back up to 1/2 cup with more Everclear. Since there will mostly likely be some particulate after the cheesecloth treatment, it is recommended to put the liquid through a strainer, then again through a coffee filter with a funnel, which can be dripped directly into a 1 liter container of choice. Once the herb-infused alcohol has been placed in the final container, add in the Splenda, water, brandy, and red wine vinegar.*

*Warning: Using high proof food-grade grain alcohol (Everclear) can be dangerous. It is highly flammable and should never be imbibed by itself as inebriation can happen very quickly and much faster than one would expect. Everclear is odorless and tasteless, which makes it ideal for our purposes, but makes it dangerous to leave unattended around animals or minors. Never use laboratory grade alcohol as a substitute. It can contain methanol that is highly toxic and potentially fatal. If you only have access to the higher proof 191, just substitute 3/4 cup of 191-Everclear plus 1/4 cup water for every cup of 151-proof required.

Vermouth (Sweet)

Sweet Vermouth (also known as Italian Vermouth in older cocktail books) has a long history. The origin of the word Vermouth is actually a variation on the German *Wermut*, which translates into wormwood. Of the two types, sweet and dry, sweet came about first, back in 1786, and was meant to be medicinal, with its herb-infused wine. After a time, it became more standardized and entered the world of cocktails. Regular Sweet Vermouth is actually very easy to make, as it just takes some wine, herbs, and a bit of brandy to fortify it. There are several sources on the Internet outlining how to make both sweet and dry versions.

However, due to our mission of making sugar free versions, wine is forbidden due to its sugar content. The solution is brandy. Brandy has an interesting history and was the old basis for the proof of alcohol. Upon the advent of distillation, shipping companies distilled wine, presumably hoping to reduce volume and shipping fees, and stored the distillate in barrels. The thought was to add water back to reconstitute it back to wine at the end of its journey. This idea was quickly abandoned once it was discovered that brandy is delicious and the rest, as they say, is history. After some significant research and tinkering, we used the same theories from years ago regarding the practice of reconstituting brandy into wine, then added herbs and sweetener. Most of the ingredients can be found in any grocery store; however, others had to be special ordered from Starwest Botanicals.

(continued)

Ingredients:

- Peel of half an Orange (removing as much zest as possible)
- 1 Cinnamon Stick (broken in half)
- 4 Cardamom Pods (gently crushed and not to be confused with cardamom spice)
- 1/4 Star Anise
- 1/2 tspn dried Lavender
- 1/4 tspn Wormwood
- 1/2 tspn dried Chamomile (not the tea blend)
- 1/2 cup Splenda
- 1 cup E&J Brandy (recommended for end product flavor)
- 3.5 cups Water
- 1/2 cup Everclear 151 (75% Ethanol)* (plus a little more for later)
- 8.5 tspn Red Wine Vinegar (unsweetened)

Take the orange rind and herbs and place in a sealable glass container and add the Everclear, making sure that all the contents are submerged. Place in a dark location at room temperature for 24 hours, gently swirling every few hours.

Once the herbs are done steeping, pour contents into cheesecloth over a bowl and squeeze as much herb-infused alcohol out as possible. Measure the alcohol volume. If it is less than the starting volume of half a cup, which is should be due to absorption into the herbs, add back enough volume to bring it back to half a cup. There may still be some particulate left over after the cheesecloth step. Then filter by pouring through a standard strainer, then restrain the herb-infused alcohol through a coffee filter. Place a large-mouthed funnel in the final collection bottle, and place a coffee filter in it and allow it to drip through. Once the herb-infused alcohol is in a bottle that can hold one liter of volume, add the water, Splenda, brandy, and the vinegar. Store in a cool dry location.

*Warning: Using high proof food-grade grain alcohol (Everclear) can be dangerous. It is highly flammable and should never be imbibed by itself as inebriation can happen very quickly and much faster than one would expect. Everclear is odorless and tasteless, which makes it ideal for our purposes, but makes it dangerous to leave unattended around animals or minors. Never use laboratory grade alcohol as a substitute. It can contain methanol that is highly toxic and potentially fatal. If you only have access to the higher proof 191, just substitute 3/4 cup of 191-Everclear plus 1/4 cup water for every cup of 151-proof required.

Sugar Free Cocktail Recipes

Please note that if no instructions are listed below the recipes, then add everything to a shaker cup with ice, cap, shake vigorously, then strain into a glass and enjoy!

<u>In this book</u>:

tspn = Teaspoon

Tbsn = Tablespoon

oz = ounce

Alto Cucina

Source: Stephen Shellenberger Dante (via kindredcocktails.com)

- 1 oz Scotch (Balvenie recommended)
- 1 oz Sugar Free Dry Vermouth
- 1/2 oz Sugar Free Elderflower Cordial
- 1/2 oz Sugar Free Amaro
- 1 twist Orange Peel (as garnish)

Add everything together, strain into a low ball glass, then garnish.

Angostura Fizz (or Trinidad Fizz)

Source: Bitters: A Spirited History of a Classic Cure-All, with Cocktails, Recipes, and Formulas, by Brad Thomas Parsons.

The text of the book states that the original recipe that this was adapted from appeared in the "Special Drinks for the Soda Fountain and Other Recipes" section of the 1908 *Dr. Siegert's Angostura Bitters* recipe booklet but did not reach much fame until included in the famous Baker's 1946 book *The Gentleman's Companion: Volume 2.*

- 1 oz Angostura Bitters
- 1 oz ReaLime
- 1/2 tspn Splenda
- 1/4 oz Sugar Free Simple Syrup
- 1/4 oz Sugar Free Grenadine
- 1/2 oz Heavy Whipping Cream
- 1 Egg White*
- Seltzer Water

Combine the bitters, ReaLime, Splenda syrup, grenadine, cream, and egg white in a small shaker. Cap it and give it a 10 second shake WITHOUT ICE. This should be just enough to combine the egg and cream. Now add a few cubes of ice shake until fully chilled. Strain (or double strain if extra clumpy) into a chilled martini or coupe glass. Top off with the seltzer water.

*Pasteurized eggs are recommended here, as there is no actual alcohol in this cocktail.

Apparent Sour

Source: Bobby Huegel of the Anvil Bar & Refuge in Houston, Texas.

- 1.5 oz Sugar Free Amaro
- 3/4 oz Sugar Free Elderflower Cordial
- 3/4 oz ReaLime
- 1 sprig Fresh Rosemary

Add all the ingredients in a mixing cup with some ice and give it a good shake. Strain it into a cocktail glass. Garnish with smacked rosemary.

Army & Navy

Source: Serious Eats.

- 2 oz Gin
- 0.5 oz Orgeat Syrup
- 0.25 oz ReaLemon

Aviation Cocktail

The Sugar Free Aviation Cocktail is an old one that dates back to 1916, where Hugo Ensslin first published it in Recipes for Mixed Drinks. It was also later published in the Savoy Cocktail Book, where it inexplicably omits the very necessary Crème de Violette. It's also rumored that it was named because its color resembles that of the sky. There is a wonderful history and review of the Aviation over at Cold Glass, written by Doug Ford. This cocktail works well with a more floral gin, like Bombay Sapphire.

- 1.5 oz Gin
- 3/4 oz ReaLemon
- 1/4 oz Sugar Free Maraschino Liqueur
- 1/4 oz Sugar Free Creme de Violette
- Optional: Splenda to taste (up to 1/4 teaspoon)

Basil Gin Gimlet

- 2 oz Gin
- 0.5 oz ReaLemon or ReaLime*
- 0.5 oz Sugar Free Simple Syrup
- 3–4 Basil Leaves

First, add the citrus to the syrup, and then muddle 2–3 leaves of basil. You'll want to bruise the leaves, being careful not to tear them. Shake with ice, then strain. Use another basil leaf as garnish.

*It really works either way with the ReaLemon or ReaLime. Both taste great, but each gives it a slightly different spin.

Black Rose

- 2 oz Bourbon
- 1 dash Sugar Free Grenadine
- 2 dashes Peychaud's Bitters
- 1 twist of Lemon Peel (garnish)

Fill an old fashioned glass 3/4 full of ice, then add everything, stir, then add the twist of lemon peel over the glass to express the oils in the lemon.

Blue Moon

- 2 oz Gin
- 1/2 oz Sugar Free Crème de Violette (or Crème Yvette)
- 1/2 oz ReaLemon
- 1 Egg White*
- 1/4 tspn Splenda
- 1 twist Lemon Peel (optional as garnish)

*When using an egg white, you can put it and the gin in a little dish together to help sterilize it if it is not pasteurized.

Bohemian Cocktail

Cocktail Virgin claims that Misty Kalkofen over at the Green Street Grill created this cocktail back in 2008. However, you can also find the recipe reported at St. Germain's website.

- 1 oz Sugar Free Elderflower Liqueur
- 1 oz Light Pink Grapefruit Juice*
- 1 dash Peychaud's Bitters
- 1 oz Gin

*This cocktail, while being no sugar added, does suffer from the juice problem, in which juice is normally loaded with sugar. We use Light Grapefruit Juice, which, via the product information, contains only 10g of carbohydrates per 8 ounce serving. As we are only using an ounce (or 2 ounces if you would like to double the recipe), it calculates to only 0.125g of carbohydrates (0.25g for the 2x) per serving, which is fairly negligible.

Buster Brown

Source: Kindred Cocktails. The Buster Brown is a simple variation on the Whiskey Sour.

- 1.5 oz Bourbon
- 0.5 oz ReaLemon
- 0.5 oz Sugar Free Simple Syrup
- 2 dashes Orange bitters

Place all ingredients in a shaker, add some ice, put the top on, give it a good shake, and strain.

Carolina Julep

Source: Imbibe!

- 2 oz Apple Brandy (Laird's)
- 1 oz Rye Whiskey
- 1/2 oz Sugar Free Simple Syrup
- 10 Mint Leaves

Muddle 9 mint leaves (reserving one) gently in the syrup in the bottom of a double old fashioned glass. Fill the glass with crushed ice, and then add the apple brandy and rye. Stir it a bit with a spoon, garnish with that extra mint leaf, and add a straw if desired.

Castle Habour Special

Source: Originally from 1928 and was first referenced in *The Gentleman's Companion,* by Charles H. Baker, Jr. While the cocktail calls for aged rum, spiced rum can be substituted (be aware that some spiced rums are sweetened).

- 0.5 oz Pineapple Vodka
- 1 oz ReaLime
- 1.5 oz Aged or Spiced Rum
- 3/4 oz White Rum (Bacardi)
- 1 tspn Sugar Free Grenadine
- 1/2 tspn Splenda

Place all of the components into a mixing cup, add some ice, and shake. Now pour everything onto some cubed ice and add a straw if you like.

Charles Cocktail

Source: DrinksMixer.com

- 1.5 oz Cognac/Brandy
- 1.5 oz Sugar Free Sweet Vermouth
- 1 dash Bitters

Any bitters can be used here. Play around with some different ones and see which ones you like best.

Chinese Cocktail

Source: Savoy Cocktail Book.

- 1 oz Jamaican Rum (though white or aged could be used)
- 3/4 oz Sugar Free Grenadine
- 3 dashes Sugar Free Triple Sec
- 3 dashes Sugar Free Maraschino Liqueur
- 1 dash Angostura Bitters

Add all the ingredients in a mixing cup with some ice and give it a good shake. Strain it into a cocktail glass.

Conquistador

Source: Originally created by Sam Ross, this recipe was adapted from the one found on Kindred Cocktails.

- 1 oz Tequila
- 1 oz Anejo Rum (Pyrat)
- 3/8 oz ReaLemon
- 3/8 oz ReaLime
- 1.25 oz Sugar Free Simple Syrup
- 2 dashes Orange Bitters
- 1 Egg White*

*When using an egg white, you can put it and the gin in a little dish together to help sterilize it if it is not pasteurized.

Coquito

Source: Coquito!

- 10 Dried Cloves
- 2 Cinnamon Sticks
- 2 cups Unsweetened Coconut Milk
- 2 tablespoons Splenda

Add cloves, cinnamon sticks, and coconut milk into a pan, slowly bring it up to a boil, then allow it to simmer for 30 minutes. Allow to cool, and then stir in the Splenda.   This is a non-alcoholic cocktail. However, an ounce of bourbon or brandy may spice things up a little!

Curacao Punch

Source: *Vintage Spirits and Forgotten Cocktails*, by Dr. Cocktail (Ted Haigh)—though this was originally published in 1882 by Harry Johnson's *New and Improved Bartender's Manual*

- 2–3 dashes ReaLemon
- 1/2 Tbsn Splenda
- 1 oz Club Soda
- 1 oz Brandy
- 2 oz Sugar Free Triple Sec
- 1 oz Rum
- Crushed/Shaved Ice

Stir all the ingredients together and serve over crushed/shaved ice. Shaking Club Soda can be messy and dangerous.

Daiquiri (Classic)

- 2 oz White Rum (Bacardi)
- 1 oz ReaLime
- 1/2 oz Sugar Free Simple Syrup

If you find this drink too limey, you may want to add some more syrup to taste.

Deep Sea Cocktail

Source: Savoy Cocktail Book

- 1 dash Absinthe
- 1 dash Orange Bitters
- 2 oz Sugar Free Dry Vermouth
- 2 oz Old Tom Gin (recommended)
- 1 twist Lemon Peel

Eggnog

Disclaimer: This drink contains raw egg materials! Pasteurized versions are commercially available for egg whites and yolks. Alcohol kills bacteria, but if you would rather make an alcohol-free version of this, please make sure to use pasteurized products.

Source: Alton Brown and his original recipe over on the food network site

Since this recipe calls for whole milk, it cannot be 100% carbohydrate free. Using heavy cream will not work for texture reasons. That being said, it makes about 7 cups and calls for a pint of milk (16 oz), which is only a total of around 26 grams of carbohydrates, and that only constitutes about a third of the total volume of the mixture. Alternatively, you can substitute skim milk for a lower-fat drink, but you'll sacrifice some texture. That means that a one-cup serving of eggnog contains about 3.7 grams of carbohydrates. This is dramatically reduced from store-bought versions (34g). This recipe can also easily be doubled.

(Makes 6–7 cups):

- 4 Egg Yolks
- 1/3 cup Splenda, plus 1 Tbsn for later
- 1 pint Whole Milk
- 1 cup Heavy Cream
- 3 oz Bourbon
- 1 tspn Freshly Grated Nutmeg
- 4 Egg Whites

First, make sure the eggs are room temperature before separating^ and during the mixing process. Now, beat the egg yolks with a hand mixer until they lighten in color, then slowly add the 1/3 cup of Splenda. If you add too fast, you run the risk of clumps forming. *Add the milk, cream, nutmeg, and bourbon. Gently stir until it mixes. In a separate bowl, with clean mixer beaters, beat the egg whites until soft peaks are achieved. With the mixer still running, add the tablespoon of Splenda and mix until stiff peaks form. Now whisk the egg whites into the yolk mixture, chill, and serve.*

^When separating the whites from the yolk, if any yolk gets into the whites, you will not be able to get soft peaks.

El Presidente

Source: Jason Wilson, in his book Boozehound

- 1.5 oz Dark Rum
- 3/4 oz Sugar Free Dry Vermouth
- 3/4 oz Sugar Free Triple Sec
- 1/2 barspoon Sugar Free Grenadine
- 1 twist of Orange Peel

Place all of the liquids in a mixing cup, add some ice, and then stir. Strain the cocktail into a martini glass. Zest a little orange peel over the cocktail so that the oils are expressed onto the drink, and then drop the peel into the drink.

Fool Moon

Source: Ted Haigh's *Vintage Spirits and Forgotten Cocktails*

- 2 oz Gin
- 3/4 oz Sugar Free Simple Syrup
- 1/2 oz ReaLemon
- 1 tspn Sugar Free Creme de Violette (Yvette)
- 4 Mint Leaves

Clap the mint leaves between your hands, then combine all ingredients with ice, shake, then strain out the remaining ice and mint leaves.

Gazette Cocktail

Source: Savoy Cocktail Book

- 1.5 tspn Splenda
- 1 tspn ReaLemon
- 2 oz Sugar Free Sweet Vermouth
- 2 oz Brandy/Cognac

Gold Baron

Source: Thomas Waugh over at Death + Co., in NYC

- 1/2 oz Applejack (Laird's)
- 1.5 oz Bourbon
- 1/2 oz Sugar Free Grenadine
- 1/2 tspn Splenda
- 1 barspoon Bittermens Burlesque Bitters

Stir all ingredients in an old-fashioned glass and serve on the rocks.

Gold Cup (Clio Version)

Source: Adapted from Todd Maul, Clio, in Boston (based on the "Beachbum" Berry recipe from the Hukilau Room in the Captain's Inn located in Long Beach, California.)

- 1.5 oz Rum
- 1.5 oz ReaLime
- 1/2 oz Sugar Free Maraschino Liqueur
- 1/4 oz Sugar Free Orgeat Syrup
- 1/4 oz Sugar Free Simple Syrup
- 1/4 tspn Absinthe
- 2 Mint Leaves

Add all the ingredients in a mixing cup with some ice and give it a good shake. Strain it into a cocktail glass on the rocks, then garnish with the mint leaves.

Goodnight Gracie

Source: Katie Loeb at the Oyster House in Philadelphia

- 2 oz Light Rum
- 3/4 oz Sugar Free Simple Syrup
- 1/3 oz Sugar Free Crème de Violette
- 0.5 oz ReaLime
- 1 oz water

Add all ingredients into a shaker cup over ice. Shake until your hands get cold, then strain into a martini glass.

Good Night, Irene

Source: Adapted from Audrey Saunders, from the Pegu Club in New York City.

- 1.5 oz Bourbon (Maker's Mark recommended)
- 1.5 oz Amaro

Add all the ingredients in a mixing cup with some ice and give it a good shake. Strain it into a cocktail glass with crushed ice.

Grasshopper^

- 1 oz Sugar Free Crème de Menthe
- 1 oz Sugar Free Crème de Cacao^
- 1 oz Heavy Cream
- (Optional) Green Food Coloring

Add all the reagents in a shaker tin over ice (and add the extra green food coloring, if desired) *and shake it up real good. Strain into a chilled martini glass and enjoy!* The only regrettable thing about the Sugar Free Grasshopper is that there isn't another one ready to go when you finish the first one! Enjoy (with the appropriate moderation of course)!

^The recipe calls for a white crème de cacao; however, the sugar free crème de cacao is brown in color, so it turned the sugar free grasshopper slightly brownish. If you'd rather have a green version, just add a few extra drops of green food coloring while you're mixing up the cocktail.

Gruff and Rumble

Source: Adapted from Dan Chadwick (via kindredcocktails.com), which was originally based on the original Rough and Tumble by Chris Amirault (eGullet).

- 2 oz Rum
- 1/2 oz Sugar Free Triple Sec
- 1/4 oz ReaLime
- 1 tspn Sugar Free Amaro
- 1 dash Fee Brothers Whiskey Barrel Aged Bitters

Add all the ingredients in a mixing cup with some ice and give it a good shake. Strain it into a cocktail glass.

Hawaiian Room

Source: Ted Saucier's *Bottom's Up,* circa 1951

- 1 oz Light Rum
- 0.5 oz Applejack (Laird's)
- 0.5 oz Pineapple Vodka
- 0.5 oz Sugar Free Triple Sec
- 0.5 oz ReaLemon
- 1 tspn Splenda

Add all your liquids on ice in a shaker, add the Splenda, and shake! Strain into a martini glass.

Hershey Manhattan^

Source: kindredcocktails.com

- 3 oz Bourbon
- 1.5 oz Sugar Free Sweet Vermouth
- 2 Tbsn Sugar Free Crème de Cacao

Mix all ingredients into a double old fashioned glass over ice and stir.

^This is enough to make two cocktails. Halve it if drinking solo, as a standard cocktail only contains 2 ounces of liquor.

Hong Kong Cocktail

Source: The original recipe can be found on the Kindred Cocktails website.

- 1 oz Gin
- 1 oz Sugar Free Dry Vermouth
- 1/2 oz ReaLime
- 2 tspn Sugar Free Simple Syrup
- 1 dash Orange Bitters

Hot Toddy

- 2 oz Brandy
- 4 oz Hot Water
- 1 level tspn Splenda
- Freshly Grated Nutmeg

Mix all ingredients together in a heat-resistant mug, except the nutmeg. Freshly grate the nutmeg directly on top of the drink before serving.

Imperial Fizz (aka the Whiskey Fizz)

Sources: Drinksmixer, or Savoy, Savoy Stomp

- 1/2 oz Light Rum
- 1.5 oz Blended Whiskey
- 1 oz ReaLemon
- 2 tspn Splenda
- Soda Water

Add the rum, whiskey, ReaLemon, and Splenda over ice in a shaker bottom, cap, and give it a good shake. Strain out the ice and pour into a double old-fashioned glass. Top off with some soda water.

Lion's Tail

- 2 oz Bourbon
- 0.5 oz Sugar Free Allspice Dram
- 0.5 oz ReaLime
- 1 tspn Sugar Free Simple Syrup
- 1 dash Angostura Bitters

Put some ice in a shaker, pour in all your components, top it, shake it for at least 10 seconds, and strain it into a cocktail glass.

Magnolia Blossom

Source: Savoy Cocktail Book

- 1 oz ReaLemon
- 2 tspn Splenda
- 1 oz Heavy Cream
- 2 oz Gin
- 1 dash Sugar Free Grenadine

Margarita

- 2 oz Silver Tequila
- 1 oz Sugar Free Triple Sec
- 0.5 oz ReaLime
- 0.5 oz Water
- Large Grain Sea Salt
- Ice*

Mix and shake the components and pour into a salt-rimmed martini glass.

*This can be served with or without ice, depending on personal preference. If you do chill, don't shake too long or you risk over-diluting your flavors.

Margarita Violette

- 1.5 oz Tequila
- 1 oz Sugar Free Triple Sec
- 1/4 oz Sugar Free Crème de Violette
- 1/2 oz ReaLime
- 1/4 tspn Splenda
- Large Grain Sea Salt

Mix and shake the ingredients and pour into a salt-rimmed martini glass.

Mark Twain Cocktail^

Source: *The Craft of the Cocktail: Everything You Need to Know to Be a Master Bartender, with 500 Recipes*, by Dale DeGroff

- 1.5 oz Blended Scotch
- 3/4 oz ReaLemon
- 1 oz Sugar Free Simple Syrup
- 2 dashes Angostura Bitters

Shake all ingredients with ice and strain into chilled cocktail glass.

^The cocktail gets its name due to a letter that Mr. Twain wrote his wife from London in January of 1864 (and quoted from *Mark and Livy: The Love Story of Mark Twain and the Woman Who Almost Tamed Him*, by Resa Willis):

"Livy my darling, I want you to be sure & remember to have, in the bathroom, when I arrive, a bottle of Scotch whiskey, a lemon, some crushed sugar, & a bottle of Angostura bitters. Ever since I have been in London I have taken in a wine glass what is called a cock-tail (made with those ingredients) before breakfast, before dinner, & just before going to bed."

Means of Preservation

Source: Adapted from John Gertsen's recipe (found on kindredcocktails.com).

- 2 oz Gin
- 1/2 oz Sugar Free Elderflower Cordial
- 1/2 oz Sugar Free Dry Vermouth
- 2 dashes Celery Bitters
- 1 twist Grapefruit Peel

Add all the ingredients in a mixing cup with some ice and give it a good shake. Strain it into a cocktail glass. Garnish with the grapefruit peel, making sure to express some of the oils over the drink.

Metropole

Source: Looka website (run by Chuck Taggart). This particular recipe originally called for equal parts brandy and dry vermouth, but this recipe was modified from a book published in 1904 called *Drinks as They Are Mixed,* by Paul E. Lowe.

- 1.5 oz Brandy
- 0.75 oz Sugar Free Dry Vermouth
- 0.5 oz Sugar Free Simple Syrup
- 2 dashes Peychaud's Bitters
- 1 dash Orange Bitters

Mexican Firing Squad

Source: kindredcocktails.com—however, the original is credited to the Raines Law Room back in 2010. There is an interesting addition in the comments section of Kindred Cocktails that the real origin of the drink has much older roots. It specifically mentions a book called The Gentleman's Companion vol. 2, by Charles H. Baker (1939).

- 2 oz Blanco Tequila
- 3/4 oz ReaLime
- 3/4 oz Sugar Free Grenadine
- 2 dashes Angostura Bitters
- 1/2 tspn Splenda
- ~1 oz Soda Water
- (Optional: 1 Wedge of Lime for Garnish)

Add all the ingredients into a shaker tin with ice, except the soda water. NOTE: Do not add the soda water at this point, as it will make a horrible mess! Cap and shake until well mixed. Add fresh ice to a Collins glass or a single old fashioned glass, then strain the mixed ingredients into it. Top off with the soda water.

Mississippi Punch

Source: Esquire Magazine

- 2 oz Cognac
- 1 oz Dark Rum
- 1 oz Bourbon
- 0.5 oz ReaLemon
- 2 tspn Splenda

Mojito

Source: allrecipes.com

- 1.5oz Rum
- 10 Mint Leaves
- 1.5 Tbsn Splenda
- 0.5 oz ReaLime
- Whole Ice Cubes
- Seltzer Water

Measure and pour the ReaLime directly into the glass and add 7–8 mint leaves directly to the glass. Then add the Splenda and muddle. Pour on the rum and fill the glass up with ice. Then add the seltzer water until the glass is full. Insert your sprig, give it a little stir, and serve.

Mulata Daisy*

Source: The original creation, which was the winner of the 2008 Bacardi Superior Rum Legacy Cocktail Competition, was created by Angostino Perrone, who works at the Connaught Bar in London.

- 1.5 oz Light Rum
- 1 oz Sugar Free Creme de Cacao
- 2/3 oz ReaLime
- 2.5 tspn Splenda
- 1.5 tspn Fennel Seeds
- 1 rinse Sugar Free Sweet Vermouth

Place the ReaLime and the Splenda in a mixing cup. Allow the Splenda to dissolve completely, then add the fennel seeds. Crush/muddle the seeds in the mix for a minute to unlock some of the flavor. Now, add some ice and the rest of the ingredients and stir. Now double strain^ into a martini glass.

^Use a normal strainer and pour into a regular glass, then take the contents of that glass and put them through a small mesh strainer. This is advisable, as otherwise you'll end up with bits of fennel seed that stick in your teeth.

*The original recipe called for Galliano. This is an anise-base liqueur, so we just substituted Sugar Free Sweet Vermouth since they have some of the same basic flavor profiles. An absinthe rinse may also work.

Nannie Dee

- 2.5 oz Canadian Club Blended Whiskey (9 yr.)
- 0.5 oz Allspice Dram
- Lemon Zest

Add the whiskey and dram in a mixing cup, add two ice cubes, stir to taste, and strain into a glass. To get the most out of your zesting, freshly zest the lemon over the glass to get the oils. You'll know you've done this correctly if you see slightly oily drops on the surface of the liquid. Add a bit of lemon peel into the drink.

Old Fashioned Cocktail

- 1 tspn Splenda
- 2 oz Bourbon or Rye Whiskey^
- 2 dashes Angostura Bitters
- Optional (add only one) Twist of Orange, Lemon, or Bitters

With the Splenda in a mixing cup, add the spirit of choice, along with whatever bitters you've decided upon. Now add several ice cubes and shake in mixing cups. Strain into an Old Fashioned glass and enjoy!

^Disclaimer: If you do not enjoy a whiskey or rye neat, you will probably not enjoy it in an Old Fashioned, so plan your bourbon or rye use well.

Opening Cocktail

Source: Savoy Cocktail Book

- 1 oz Sugar Free Grenadine
- 1 oz Sugar Free Sweet Vermouth
- 2 oz Canadian Club Whiskey

Add all the ingredients in a mixing cup with some ice and give it a good shake. Strain it into a cocktail glass.

Paloma

Source: Imbibe Magazine

- 2 oz Hornitos Blanco or Reposado Tequila
- 0.5 oz ReaLime
- Pinch of Salt*
- ~4 oz Sugar Free Grapefruit Soda (Diet Squirt)

Place a few cubes of ice in an 8-ounce highball glass,** then pour in the tequila and ReaLime. Now add the pinch of salt and give it a little stir. Now pour in the soda until the glass is full.

*A pinch of salt can be highly subjective, but for our purposes we go by a pinch being equal to 1/8th of a teaspoon.

**Highball glasses can come in 8 or 10+ ounce varieties. If using a larger one, please take the time to measure the soda, or else the proportions will be very off.

Panama Cocktail

Source: Savoy Cocktail Book

- 1 oz Sugar Free Creme de Cacao
- 1 oz Heavy Whipping Cream
- 1 oz Brandy
- 1 tspn Splenda

Piña Colada
Source: This is an original creation of the author.

- 2 oz White Rum
- 1.5 oz Pineapple Vodka
- 1 oz Heavy Cream
- 1/4 tspn Coconut Extract
- 4 tspn Splenda
- 16 Ice Cubes (or 8 ounces)*

If possible, have the rum or vodka pre-chilled in the freezer. The proper sequence here is key. First, add the cream to a blender and a few ice cubes. Set the blender to the "auto crush" setting if it has one and let it run. Next, add the Splenda. The goal here is to froth up the cream a bit and get it whipped up to add texture and foaminess. Now add your rum. Add a few more ice cubes at this point. Since it is the ice that is providing the texture, switching back and forth between room temperature and cold reagents will minimize ice melting. Now add the coconut extract and the vodka. Keep the auto-crush going and don't stop! Once all other ingredients have been added, add the remaining ice cubes one at a time (otherwise you risk seizing up the blender). Once done, pour into a glass and enjoy. This recipe can be scaled up to make 2–3 drinks at a time.

*We used ice cubes that were 5/8 oz by weight. This is worth mentioning, because if you use smaller or larger cubes, this will change the flavor ratios, which will result in a stronger/weaker drink. Since there is no actual pineapple or coconut milk in our Sugar Free Piña Colada, the ice cubes provide the icy texture of the drink, so these ratios are very, very important!

Pink Lady

Source: Vintage Spirits and Forgotten Cocktails, by
Ted Haigh, aka Dr. Cocktail

- 1.5 oz Gin
- 0.5 oz Applejack (Laird's)
- 2 oz ReaLemon
- 1 Egg White*
- 0.5 tspn Splenda
- 2 dashes Sugar Free Grenadine

*As with all uncooked egg ingredients, we recommend
pasteurized eggs, or you can also pre-mix the alcohol with
the egg white for a couple minutes to reduce the risk of any
contamination.

Pioneer Spirit

Source: Raines Law Room in NYC. It is, as many
drinks are, an adaptation of a classic. In this case, it's
a new spin on the Old Fashioned.

- 2 dashes Angostura Bitters
- 1 barspoon (~0.8 oz) Sugar Free Orgeat Syrup
- 1.5 oz Rye Whiskey (Old Overholt)
- 0.5 oz Applejack (Lairds^)
- 1 twist Orange Peel (as garnish)

*First, add all the liquid ingredients over ice in a
mixing cup. Shake, and strain into an old fashioned
glass. Then take your peeler to an orange and cut a
small strip over the glass, spraying the oils over the
drink, then drop in the peel.*

^It should be noted that not all applejack is created equally. When we refer to applejack, we mean an apple brandy. The original applejack recipe was made using freeze distillation (or fractional freezing) of cider. This technique has fallen out of favor for newer methods, since the original distillation method could produce trace amounts of methanol, which can be deadly, but newer safe versions can sometimes be found. This old fashioned applejack is made from cider and is chock full of sugar! Be advised that if avoiding sugar, do not use this. We urge you to read labels carefully, or just go with Lairds.

Planters Punch (Simple)

Source: This version of the Sugar Free Simple Planters Punch is a variation on the recipe that was published back in 1939, according to Kindred Cocktails. Wikipedia claims that it really dates back to 1878! Any way you look at it, this drink has been around for quite a while! The original recipe calls for some orange juice, which I'm sure would give it some extra color and flavor, but goes against the low/no carb rule, so this recipe leaves our the orange juice.

- 3 oz Rum
- 0.5 oz ReaLime
- 0.5 oz ReaLemon
- 0.75 oz Sugar Free Grenadine
- 0.5 oz Sugar Free Simple Syrup

Add all the ingredients into a shaker cup. Add ice, shake, and strain into a glass.

Prescription Julep

- 1.5 oz Cognac
- 0.5 oz Rye
- 0.5 oz Sugar Free Simple Syrup
- 1.0 oz Water
- Fresh Mint (5–6 leaves)

Muddle the mint, and then add the crushed ice to fill up most of an Old Fashioned glass. Add the rest of the ingredients and stir. A straw is recommended. Can also garnish with an additional sprig of mint.

Pumpkin Spice Cocktail

Source: Original creation by the author

- 2 oz Bourbon
- 2 oz Heavy Whipping Cream
- 0.5 oz Sugar Free Allspice Dram
- 0.5 tspn Pumpkin Extract^
- 1 Tbsn Splenda
- Nutmeg (Freshly Ground)

This drink can either be served warm or cold!

Cold Version:
Take all ingredients, except the nutmeg, and combine in a medium-sized shaker tin over ice. Give the mixture some good shaking in order to really froth up that cream. Strain into a martini glass and grind a little bit of fresh nutmeg over top.

Hot Version:
Mix exactly as with the Cold Version, up until the nutmeg step (maintaining the ice requirement

guarantees that an over-boozy drink does not develop, so the ice step is still integral). Now we face the challenge of heating the cocktail without burning the cream component. This can usually be accomplished by slowly heating the mixture. A microwave is not recommended. A slow warming process should be employed. You can either transfer the cup to a pan of water and slowly raise the temperature while stirring or, if a heat-safe bottle is available, pour the cocktail into it and warm it up in a baby-bottle warmer (just remember to cap and shake to avoid hot spots!).

Once hot, transfer your cocktail into a mug and grind some nutmeg over the top.

^It is important to note that we use Pumpkin Extract and not Pumpkin Pie Extract. We wanted the pure essence of pumpkin without the tag-along flavors that may come with the pie version. Feel free to experiment with the Pumpkin Pie Extract, if you like, but be warned that the amount of Allspice Dram may need to be changed. We found that All Star Extracts (via Amazon) had one of the few pure pumpkin extracts that we could find.

Ramos Gin Fizz

Source: Sazerac Bar in the Roosevelt in New Orleans

- 1.5 oz Gin
- 1 oz ReaLemon
- 0.5 oz ReaLime
- 1 Egg White
- 2 oz Heavy Whipping Cream
- 1 oz Water
- 1 Tbsn Splenda
- 3–4 drops Orange Flower Water
  Continued

*Add the gin to the egg white in a medium shaker (this will reduce the risk of illness, but using pasteurized eggs will further reduce this risk). After a minute, add the remaining ingredients EXCEPT the heavy cream. Whether using real citrus or fake, there is a risk of curdling the cream due to the acidity. Add a handful of cracked ice, followed by the heavy cream. Cap it, then shake it harder than any drink you've ever made before!^*

^An important note about the shaking: Since this is creating an emulsion from the egg white, this will require more than a little shaking, so make sure that the tins are tight. The shakers are going to get very cold, but I would recommend shaking no less than two minutes, the more vigorous the better. Trust me, you'll be rewarded for your efforts.

Royale with Ease

Source: Esquire Magazine

- 1.5 oz Tenneyson Absinthe Royale (or any Absinthe really)
- 1.5 oz Light Grapefruit Juice^
- 1 oz Sugar Free Hibiscus Simple Syrup
- 0.5 oz ReaLime
- 0.25 oz Sugar Free Allspice Dram
- 3 dashes Angostura Bitters
- Mint Leaves
- Grapefruit Peel

Combine ingredients in a mixing glass and shake. Now strain into an ice-filled old-fashioned glass. Garnish with mint leaves and a grapefruit peel.

^The actual carb count in this drink can easily be calculated. The light grapefruit juice is 13 grams per serving, and a serving is 8 ounces. The recipe calls for 1.5 ounces, which comes to 18.75% of a serving, which comes to a net carb count of 2.44 grams. This is a little more than no carb, but should be pretty negligible.

Saint Croix Rum Fix

Source: Vintage Spirits and Forgotten Cocktails, as written by Dr. Cocktail, but was actually originally published in *The Complete Bartender,* by Albert Barnes in 1884!

- 0.5 oz Pineapple Vodka
- 2 oz Dark Rum
- 1 oz ReaLemon
- 2.5 tspn Splenda
- Crushed/Shaved Ice

Place the ice in a martini glass until it's about 3/4 full. Then, in a separate mixing cup, add all the reagents and stir until mixed. Once mixed, pour directly into your iced martini glass.

Sazerac

Source: The Sazerac Bar in the Roosevelt in New Orleans

- 2 oz Rye Whiskey
- 1/2 oz Sugar Free Simple Syrup or 1 tspn Splenda
- 2 dashes Peychaud's Bitters
- Rinse Absinthe^
- Lemon Peel

If you use simple syrup, there is no reason to muddle (continued) *and you can skip this step, but if you just want to use Splenda, measure the Splenda into an extra cup and add the bitters. Then muddle the Splenda in the bitters until it completely dissolves. Add a few cubes of ice and add the rye. Gently stir until the drink gets really cold and takes on a slight shimmer. In a separate glass (a 4 ounce glass works great), pour a little bit of absinthe in the bottom and turn the glass around until the absinthe covers all the interior glass surface, then pour out the remainder.* Then strain out the ice cubes from your first glass and the drink into the absinthe-rinsed glass. Take out your zester and peel a small strip of the lemon over the glass so that the oils are expressed on the drink and the small bit of peel falls into the glass.*

^There is a long history of absinthe being the original rinse agent of this cocktail, however, as we've learned, when absinthe was banned in 1915 in the USA, Sazerac makers in New Orleans switched over to Herbsaint after Prohibition ended in 1934. We actually asked the bartender in the Sazerac Bar why he was using Herbsaint instead of Absinthe and he told us that even though the drink originated with absinthe, Herbsaint has been used longer that absinthe ever was, so it's just become the standard. Herbsaint is an anise-based liqueur, so it has that flavor in common with absinthe, so it was a reasonable substitution. However, since all liqueurs are sweetened, and our goal is sugar free, so we used the no sugar-containing absinthe (which is no longer banned and has been commercially available since 2000).

*If you are making more than one, don't waste that precious absinthe. Just pour the post-rinse remainder into the next glass.

Scofflaw

Source: Vintage Spirits & Forgotten Cocktails, by Ted Haigh (Dr. Cocktail) and the Savoy Cocktail Book. Gavin Duffy originally created this drink in the Harry's New York Bar in Paris.

Not only is it a delicious vintage recipe from 1924, but it also has a little bit of interesting history. This drink was created during Prohibition. The Scofflaw's name originates from the word scofflaw, which literally means "one who flouts laws." Also, the term itself was coined from a contest during Prohibition, in which 25,000 entries were submitted in order to come up with a word for those that liked to partake of alcohol during this time (and oddly enough, two separate people submitted the same word and ended up splitting the $200 prize). The naming of the drink was a direct snub at the American government by the Parisians.

- 1.5 oz Rye
- 1 oz Sugar Free Dry Vermouth
- 3/4 oz ReaLemon
- 3/4 oz Sugar Free Grenadine
- 3/4 tspn Splenda
- 1 twist Lemon Peel (garnish)

Add all the ingredients, except the lemon peel, over ice in a small shaker cup. Add the topper, shake vigorously, then strain into a martini glass. Add a twist of fresh lemon peel over the top, being careful to express some of the oils into the drink.

Smoky Grove

Source: The PDT Cocktail Book

- 2 oz Blended Scotch (the more peat flavor the better)
- 1/2 oz Sugar Free Sweet Vermouth
- 1/2 oz Sugar Free Dry Vermouth
- 1 dash Angostura Bitters
- 1 dash Orange Bitters
- 1 twist Orange Peel^

Place all the ingredients, except the orange peel, into a mixing cup with ice. Stir it until it is very cold, then strain into a martini glass. Next, take an orange and cut a small sliver with a twist knife, making sure that the oils of the orange spray out over the drink. Then allow the peel to drop into the glass.

^This drink remains totally Sugar Free, despite the small use of orange peel. The peel itself contains such an infinitesimal amount of carbohydrate, and since we are using less than a gram of peel, the amount included can just be ignored.

Solstice

Source: @mahastew (aka Stew Ellington), who is the author of 901 Very Good Cocktails: A Practical Guide

- 0.75 oz Sugar Free Triple Sec
- 2 oz Rye
- 0.25 oz Sugar Free Allspice Dram

Add ice to a glass; add all the reagents, stir, and serve.

Special Relationship

Source: kindred cocktails user endless_optimism, though we are uncertain as to who this user really is or if they have a twitter account (we couldn't find one)

- 1/2 oz Rye
- 1/2 oz Bourbon
- 1/2 oz Blended Scotch
- 1/2 oz Applejack (Laird's)
- 1/4 oz Sugar Free Simple Syrup
- 2 dashes Orange Bitters (barrel aged is recommended)
- 1 dash Angostura Bitters
- 1 barspoon^ Scotch (Laphroaig)
- 1 twist Orange Peel
- 1 twist Lemon Peel

Combine all of the different reagents, except for the orange and lemon garnishes, with ice. Stir well and strain into an old fashioned glass with (preferably) a large ice rock. Cut and twist the orange and lemon, dropping the twists into the cocktail, making sure to express the oils over the drink first.

^While a barspoon does hold the same volume as a standard teaspoon (5mL), its function is a little different for a bartender. It can be used to stir the entire length of any sized mixer or glass, and its twisting length can be used for carefully layering small amounts of liquid into a cocktail.

Stinger

Source: Tom Bullock's *Ideal Bartender,* which was published back in 1917. There are also two ways to make the Sugar Free Stinger, one shaken and strained and the other poured over crushed ice. For our palettes, the crushed ice version was definitely a lot less strong. However, if you like your brandy, feel free to drink it without the ice.

- 3 oz Cognac/Brandy
- 1/4 oz Sugar Free Creme de Menthe

Option 1: *Pour both ingredients together over ice and shake, and then strain into a martini glass.* This method results in a stronger drink.^

Option 2: *Pour both ingredients together over ice and shake, and then strain into a double old-fashioned glass filled with crushed ice. Insert a straw and serve.* This method results in a mellower cocktail, which stays colder longer.

^If Option 1 turns out to be too strong, it can easily be converted into Option 2.

Tango 'til They're Sore

Source: Adapted from Rafa Garcin Febles' recipe, based out of New York City (via kindredcocktails.com).

- 1 oz Rye
- 3/4 oz Sugar Free Sweet Vermouth
- 1/2 oz Sugar Free Maraschino Liqueur
- 3/4 oz Peychaud's Bitters
- 1 twist Orange Peel

Add all the ingredients in a mixing cup with some ice and give it a good shake. Strain it into a cocktail glass. Garnish with the orange peel, making sure to express some of the oils over the drink. Note, that is three quarters of an ounce of bitters, which is generally a lot more than is normal in a cocktail.

Tom Collins

Source: Created back in 1876 by the famous bartender, Jerry Thomas. It's believed that Jerry Thomas based this drink on the Great Tom Collins Hoax of 1874.

- 1 oz ReaLemon
- 1 oz Sugar Free Simple Syrup
- Soda Water (to top off)
- 2 oz Gin
- 1 tspn Splenda
- 2 dashes Angostura Bitters*

(continued)

Add the Simple Syrup, the lemon, Splenda, and gin to a shaker cup with ice (and Angostura, if you like). *Cap it and give it a few shakes until the cup gets cold. Add more ice to the glass, and then strain the contents of the shaker into the glass. Now top with soda water. Give it a little stir, and serve.*

*The Angostura is not part of the regular recipe but something we added to give the drink a little extra flavor. It turned out really wonderfully, and we highly recommend it! However, the bitters are completely optional.

Trans-Siberian Express

Source: Adapted from Rafa Garcin Febles' recipe, based out of New York City (via kindredcocktails.com).

- 1.5 oz Gin
- 3/4 oz ReaLime
- 1/2 oz Sugar Free Amaro
- 1/4 oz Sugar Free Crème de Menthe
- 1 barspoon Crème de Cacao
- 2 dashes Orange Bitters
- 1 sprig Fresh Mint

Add all the ingredients in a mixing cup with some ice and give it a good shake. Strain it into a cocktail glass. Garnish with the mint.

Trinidad Sour

Source: Adapted from Giuseppe Gonzalez's recipe from the Clover Club, Brooklyn, New York (via kindredcocktails.com).

- 1 oz Angostura Bitters
- 1 oz Sugar Free Orgeat Syrup
- 3/4 oz ReaLemon
- 1/2 oz Rye

Add all the ingredients in a mixing cup with some ice and give it a good shake. Strain it into a cocktail glass. Note: That is a full ounce of bitters. Angostura is providing most the alcohol in this cocktail.

Whiskey Sour

Source: Imbibe! Magazine

- 2 oz Bourbon Whiskey
- 1 oz Water
- 1 tspn Sugar Free Simple Syrup
- 1 oz ReaLemon
- Optional: Red Wine*

Pour all the ingredients into a shaker, add ice, put the lid on your shaker, give it 5–10 seconds of shaking, and strain into your glass of choice.

*I try to stay away from all wines. For whatever reason, the sugar in the wine disrupts my blood sugars. However, for all the imbibers out there who don't have the same sugar problems that I do, a classy option is to take a little bit of red wine and float it on the top. Take a bar spoon (or a teaspoon) and turn it upside down. Then carefully pour a little of the wine onto the spoon, directing the flow on the top of the drink to make a layer of wine. This is more difficult than it seems and may require some practice before getting it right. If it fails and mixes, oh well, just drink it and try again! And as a side note, if you prefer, rye whiskey can be substituted for bourbon.

Wild Hibiscus Sour

Source: BarNoneDrinks.com

- 2 oz Bourbon
- 1 oz ReaLime
- 1 oz Pineapple Vodka
- 1.5 oz Sugar Free Hibiscus Syrup
- 1 tspn Splenda
- 1 Egg White*

Add all the alcohol and egg white into a medium mixing cup, stir, and allow to sit for a minute. Then add ice and cover with a large shaker top. Give it some serious shaking. In a double old fashioned glass, add three or four cubes of ice, then strain your shaken cocktail over the ice. If desired, let it settle for a minute, and some of the foam will make a pretty layer on top.

*As always, use pasteurized eggs or mix the egg white with the bourbon to reduce the risks of contamination.

Woody Sour

Source: Daniel Rutkowski

- 1.5 oz Bourbon
- 3/4 oz Rye
- 3/4 oz ReaLemon
- 1/2 oz Sugar Free Simple Syrup
- 1/4 oz Sugar Free Allspice Dram
- 2 dashes Fee Brothers Whiskey Barrel Aged Bitters
- 1 peel Lemon Zest

Add all the ingredients in a small shaker cup over ice. Place some fresh ice in a single old-fashioned glass. Cap and shake, then strain into the ice-filled glass! Then zest the lemon over the glass, letting the oils drop into the glass. Serve.

ABOUT THE AUTHOR

Scott Reba has been a Type 1 Diabetic for over 25 years. Wanting to enjoy drinks with family and friends, he founded mixdrinkrepeat.com to catalog his journey into developing the techniques to create and enjoy Sugar Free Cocktails. Scott has been a lifelong Cleveland-area resident, where he lives with his wife, two kids, a crazy puppy, and a cat. In his day job, he works as a research laboratory manager at Case Western Reserve University.

INDEX

Made in United States
Orlando, FL
15 April 2022

16881572R00064